Searchlight BOOKS™

How Do Simple Machines Work?

Put Levers to the Test

by Sally M. Walker and Roseann Feldmann

Lerner Publications Company
Minneapolis

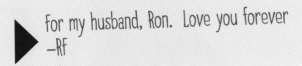

For my husband, Ron. Love you forever
—RF

Lerner Publications Company
A division of Lerner Publishing Group, Inc.
241 First Avenue North
Minneapolis, MN 55401 U.S.A.

Website address: www.lernerbooks.com

Library of Congress Cataloging-in-Publication Data

Walker, Sally M.
        Put levers to the test / by Sally M. Walker and Roseann Feldmann.
            p.   cm. — (Searchlight books™—How do simple machines work?)
        Includes index.
        ISBN 978–0–7613–5321–8 (lib. bdg. : alk. paper)
        1. Levers—Juvenile literature. I. Feldmann, Roseann. II. Title.
    TJ147.W36 2012
    621.8—dc22   2010035551

Manufactured in the United States of America
1 – DP – 7/15/11

2

Contents

Chapter 1

WORK

You work every day. You do chores around your home. At school you write. It may surprise you to learn that playing and eating are work too!

You do work when you write. What does the word *work* mean to a scientist?

Work = Using Force to Move an Object

When scientists use the word *work*, they don't mean the opposite of play. Work is using force to move an object from one place to another. Force is a push or a pull. You use force to carry out the trash. And you use force to turn the page of a book.

You do work when you take out the trash.

Every time you use force, the force has a direction. Force can move in any direction. When you push open a door, the force is aimed away from you.

The direction of a force can be away from you.

You use an upward force to open some kinds of windows. And you use a downward force when you type on a computer.

You use a downward force when you type.

You do work when you move sand from one place to another place.

Throwing a Ball Is Work

Every time your force moves an object, you have done work. It doesn't matter how far the object moves. If it moves, work has been done. Throwing a ball is work. Your force moves the ball from one place to another.

Pushing a Building Is NOT Work!

Pushing your school building is not work. It's not work if you sweat. It's not work even if you push until your arms feel like rubber. No matter how hard you push, you haven't done work. The building hasn't moved. If the building moves, then you worked!

These kids are pushing very hard on a school building. But they are not doing work.

Chapter 2

MACHINES

Most people want their work to be easy. Machines are tools that make work easier.

Complicated Machines

Some machines have many moving parts. These machines are called complicated machines. Cars and vacuum cleaners are complicated machines.

A vacuum cleaner is a machine that has many moving parts. What kind of machine is it?

Simple Machines

Some machines have only a few moving parts. These machines are called simple machines. Simple machines are found in every home, school, and playground. They are so simple that you might not realize they are machines.

A light switch is a simple machine.

Simple machines make work easier in many ways. One way is by changing the direction of force. When you use your arms to lift a friend, you use an upward force. But you can lift your friend more easily by using a downward force. How?

Lifting a friend is hard.

The girl on the right sits on one end of the seesaw. The other end of the seesaw goes up and lifts her friend.

If your friend sits on a seesaw, the end your friend sits on goes down. When you sit on the other end, your friends goes up. Your force is downward. But your friend still goes up.

Chapter 3

PARTS OF A LEVER

The seesaw is a simple machine. This kind of simple machine is called a lever. A lever is a bar that is hard to bend. Levers make it easier to move things.

A bottle opener is a simple machine called a lever. What do levers help people to do?

14

A lever must rest on another object. The object a lever rests on is called its fulcrum. You can make a lever.

What You Need
You will need a 12-inch (30-centimeter) wooden ruler, a crayon, a small can of food, and some rubber bands.

YOU CAN USE THESE OBJECTS TO MAKE YOUR OWN LEVER.

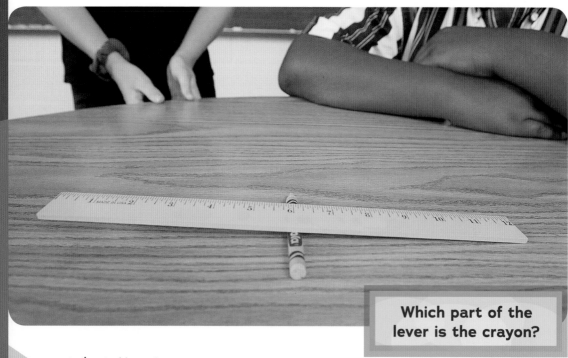

Which part of the lever is the crayon?

What You Do

Place the ruler on the crayon. Put the crayon under the ruler's 6-inch (15 cm) mark. One end of the ruler will probably touch the table. The ruler is your lever. It rests on top of the crayon. So the crayon is the ruler's fulcrum.

The ruler and the crayon work together. Push down on the high end of the ruler. What happens? Your downward force makes the other end of the ruler go up.

When you push down on one end of the lever, the other end goes up.

Put one finger on each end of the ruler. Push one end down. Then push the other end down. Watch the crayon. What happens? The crayon stays in the same place while the ruler moves around it.

The crayon is the lever's fulcrum. The lever moves, but the fulcrum stays in the same place.

Now put the can on the ruler. The middle of the can should be on top of the ruler's 11-inch (28 cm) mark. Use the rubber bands to hold the can to the ruler. The can is the lever's load. A load is an object you want to move.

The can is the lever's load.

A lever helps you lift a load.

Put the crayon under the ruler's 6-inch (15 cm) mark. Push the high end of the ruler down. Your force makes the lever move around its fulcrum. Lifting the load is easy. You don't have to use much force.

Think about It

Think about your lever. Your finger makes a force on one end of the lever. The can is the load at the other end of the lever. The crayon is the fulcrum between the load and the force.

A lever can't hold up a load without a force. If you stop pushing down on the ruler, the can crashes down.

A lever can't hold up a load without force.

Chapter 4

CHANGING THE AMOUNT OF FORCE

You can change how much force you must use to lift the can. To change the force, you must change the lever a bit.

Now Try This!

Put the crayon under your lever's 9-inch (23 cm) mark. The lever looks different now. The fulcrum is far away from your force.

The crayon is in a new place now. Will moving the crayon change how hard you have to work?

Push down on the high end. It's easy to lift the load. You need to use only a little force. Moving the fulcrum farther away from the force makes your work easier.

Next, put the crayon under the ruler's 3-inch (8 cm) mark. Now the fulcrum is close to your force. Push down on the high end of the lever. You have to use a lot of force to lift the load. Putting the fulcrum close to the force makes your work harder.

When the fulcrum is close to the force, your work is harder.

The fulcrum is close to the load again.

Does moving the fulcrum change how high the load is lifted? Put the crayon under the ruler's 9-inch (23 cm) mark. Notice how high the ruler's end is above the tabletop.

Push down on the lever to lift the load. When the can goes up, try to slide a finger under the raised end of the ruler. There's probably just enough room for your finger to fit. Your long downward push is easy. But it raises the can only a small distance.

The load is raised only a small distance.

Put the crayon back under the ruler's 3-inch (8 cm) mark. The end you will push down is much closer to the tabletop now. What happens to the load when you push down again?

This time, the fulcrum is far from the load.

The load goes up high when the fulcrum is far from the load. But lifting the load is hard.

The can goes up higher this time. You may be able to fit two fingers under the ruler's end. Your short downward push was a lot harder. But it lifted the can much higher.

Press the ruler's end halfway down. Both ends of the ruler should be above the table. Now push the ruler back and forth over the crayon. Notice how your force changes as you do this. Your force changes as your finger gets closer to or farther from the fulcrum.

AS YOUR FINGER MOVES CLOSER TO THE FULCRUM, YOU NEED TO USE MORE FORCE. AS YOUR FINGER MOVES FARTHER FROM THE FULCRUM, YOU NEED LESS FORCE.

Two Questions

When you use a lever, ask yourself two questions. Do you want to use a little force and move the load a little bit? Or do you want to use a lot of force and move the load a lot? Your answer will help you decide where to put the fulcrum. If the fulcrum is far from the force, the load moves a little. So you only need a little force. If the fulcrum is close to the force, the load moves a lot. But you must use a lot of force.

This boy is using a water pump. The handle is a lever.

Chapter 5

KINDS OF LEVERS

There are three kinds of levers. The lever you made from a ruler is one kind of lever.

First-Class Levers

The lever you made from a ruler is a first-class lever. In a first-class lever, the fulcrum is between the load and the force.

This girl is trying to lift the lid of a paint can. She is using a screwdriver as a lever. How many kinds of levers are there?

You can use a hammer to pull out a nail. When you do this, the hammer is a first-class lever.

A hammer is a first-class lever when you use it to pull out a nail. The nail is the load. The person pulling makes the force. And the fulcrum is the place where the hammer's head rests on the board. The fulcrum is between the load and the force.

Second-Class Levers

The second kind of lever is called a second-class lever. In a second-class lever, the load is between the fulcrum and the force. You can make your ruler into a second-class lever. Make sure the can is still attached at the ruler's 11-inch (28 cm) mark. Lay the ruler on the table. Put the 1-inch (2.5 cm) mark at the edge of the table. Most of the ruler will be on the table. But 1 inch will hang over the edge.

Lift the edge of the ruler several inches. Look at the lever. Can you find the fulcrum? The lever is resting on the tabletop. So the tabletop is the fulcrum. The load is between the fulcrum and the force.

Move the middle of the can to the ruler's 6-inch (15 cm) mark. Lift the end the same amount as you did before. Then move the can to the 3-inch (8 cm) mark and try it again. Do you need to use more force when the load is closer to your hand?

In a second-class lever, the load is between the fulcrum and the force.

It is harder to lift a
load when it is close
to the force.

Notice how high the can is lifted each time. When the
load is far from the force, the load moves only a little.
But it's easy to lift. When the load is close to the force,
the load moves a lot. But you need a lot of force to lift it.

A wheelbarrow is a second-class lever. The wheel is the fulcrum. The force is at the handles. The load is inside the wheelbarrow. The load is between the fulcrum and the force. When the load is toward the front of the wheelbarrow, it is easy to lift. When the load is closer to the handles, it is harder to lift.

A wheelbarrow is a
second-class lever.

Third-Class Levers

The third kind of lever is called a third-class lever. A third-class lever has the force between the fulcrum and the load.

A broom is a third-class lever. You hold the broom in two places. Your bottom arm gives the force. The top arm on the broom is the fulcrum. The dirt is the load. A third-class lever helps you move objects a long distance. A good sweep makes the broom move a long distance. You can reach out and move a lot of dirt easily.

A broom is a third-class lever.

KINDS OF LEVERS

FIRST-CLASS LEVER:
the fulcrum is between the load and the force

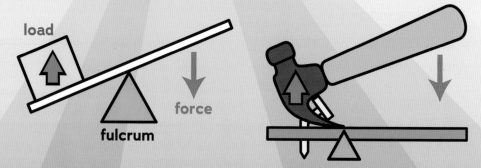

SECOND-CLASS LEVER:
the load is between the fulcrum and the force

THIRD-CLASS LEVER:
the force is between the load and the fulcrum

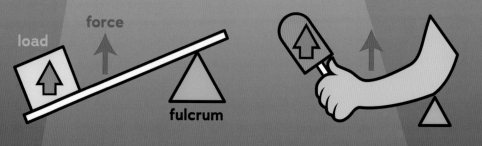

Levers Make Work Easier

Levers make doing work easier. Some levers increase your force. Some levers change the direction of your force. And some levers help you move an object a long distance.

Using a lever gives you an advantage. An advantage is a better chance of finishing your work. Using a lever is like having a helper. The work is easier. And that's a real advantage!

Pruning shears are two levers held together with a bolt. The load is far from the force. So using pruning shears makes a cutter's work easier.

Glossary

complicated machine: a machine that has many moving parts

first-class lever: a lever that has its fulcrum between the load and the force

force: a push or a pull

fulcrum: the object a lever rests on

lever: a stiff bar that is used to move other objects

load: an object you want to move

second-class lever: a lever that has its load between the fulcrum and the force

simple machine: a machine that has few moving parts

third-class lever: a lever that has its force between the fulcrum and the load

work: moving an object from one place to another

Learn More about Simple Machines

Books

Albee, Sarah. *Clever Trevor*. New York: Kane Press, 2003. This fun story tells about a boy who uses levers to get out of trouble with a bully.

Gosman, Gillian. *Levers in Action*. New York: PowerKids Press, 2011. Check out this book to see examples of levers in our everyday lives.

Walker, Sally M., and Roseann Feldmann. *Put Inclined Planes to the Test*. Minneapolis: Lerner Publications Company, 2012. Read all about inclined planes, another important simple machine.

Way, Steve, and Gerry Bailey. *Simple Machines*. Pleasantville, NY: Gareth Stevens, 2009. This title explores a variety of simple machines, from wheels and axles to ramps and levers.

Websites

Enchanted Learning: Levers
http://www.enchantedlearning.com/physics/machines/Levers.shtml
This website about levers includes animated pictures of the three types of levers.

Quia—Simple Machines
http://www.quia.com/quiz/101964.html
Visit this site to find a challenging interactive quiz that allows budding physicists to test their knowledge of simple machines.

Simple Machines
http://sln.fi.edu/qa97/spotlight3/spotlight3.html
This site features brief information about simple machines and helpful links you can click on to learn more.

Index

Photo Acknowledgments

All images provided by Andy King except for the following: © Joe McBride/Stone/Getty Images, cover; © Fuse/Getty Images, p. 5; © DK Stock/Christina Kennedy/Getty Images, p. 7; © Speedo101/Dreamstime.com, p. 8; © Celso Pupo Rodrigues/Dreamstime.com, p. 14; © Juan Carlos Lino/Alamy, p. 29; © Laura Westlund/Independent Picture Service, p. 36.

Main body text set in Adrianna Regular 14/20.
Typeface provided by Chank.

J621.8
WALKER

Walker, Sally M.

Put levers to the
test.

$27.93

J621.8
WALKER

Walker, Sally M.

Put levers to the
test.

$27.93

DATE	BORROWER'S NAME	

BAKER & TAYLOR